Endorsement for *The Deer Woman*

The temperature of the collection is cool, not chilly but critically inquisitive and able to make dramatic moments of high colour and fleshy contrast. The memorable motifs are of water and its various forms, birds and flowers, delicate things with complex constructions, a sense of Fibonacci fractals. The deer metaphor and motif is an under-note throughout, an organizing principle. The overall effect is of a poet of confidence, variety and capability.

Bonny Cassidy

The Deer Woman

Susan Fealy

Susan Fealy is a poet and clinical psychologist who lives in Melbourne on Wurundjeri land. Her poems have been published in many Australian journals, newspapers and anthologies including *The Best Australian Poems* and *Best of Australian Poems*. Her debut collection, *Flute of Milk* (UWAP) won the 2017 Wesley Michel Wright Prize, the 2018 NSW Society of Women Writers Book Award (Poetry) and shortlisted for the 2018 Association for the Study of Australian Literature Mary Gilmore Award. She has read and discussed her poetry at festivals and poetry events in Adelaide, Canberra, Melbourne, Perth and Sydney. *The Earthing of Rain* (Flying Island Books, 2019) was translated into Chinese by Iris Fan Xing.

Susan Fealy

The Deer Woman

UPSWELL

First published in Australia in 2026
by Upswell Publishing
Perth, Western Australia
upswellpublishing.com

Upswell operates in the city of Perth, on ancient country of the Whadjuk people of the Noongar nation who remain the spiritual and cultural custodians of this beautiful land. We acknowledge their continuing connection to country and express gratitude to elders past and present for their strength and creativity ... Always was, always will be, Aboriginal land.

ISBN: 978-1-7642397-5-2

A catalogue record for this book is available from the National Library of Australia

Cover image: Dapeng Liu LANDSCAPE OF THE FUTURE NO. 1 2022
61 × 51 cm, oil on canvas
Cover design by Chil3, Fremantle
Typeset in Foundry Origin by Lasertype
Printed by Lightning Source

Upswell Publishing is assisted by the State of Western Australia through its funding program for arts and culture.

Contents

IV

Individual poems in this book are dedicated to:

'*from* The Guide to Urban Living' for Debbie Lim

'Things Your Mother Never Tells You' and

'The Night Before the Truck' for Harley

'Dodge, 1960' for Alex Skovron

'A Wake of Marigolds' in memory of Retta Hemensley (1945–2021)

'The Bead' for Beverley Fealy

'Lost Oyster Buoys' for Kathryn and Ary

'A Bowerbird, Forgetting Blue' in memory of Robert Adamson (1943–2022)

For Beverley Fealy

and Ivan Fealy (1935–2025)

How easily the deer move between
the field and the woods.
Only we know a thing by its periphery

Jenny George, 'Intelligence'

The Deer Woman

after *Born*

by Kiki Smith

When a woman is born from a deer,
she arrives fully-formed.
Her breasts are round as camellias,
a soft mound declares her womb.
She is dark, as if written from the forest centre.

When a woman is born from a deer,
it begins beneath a citadel,
windows are glaciers,
the woods are a blue memory
stuttering on flood-lit screens.

When a woman is born from a deer,
a taproot grows from her throat,
it rises up through her mouth,
and she waits
for her blood to cleave and flower words.

She

In the sky a cloud goes on naming
and unnaming itself.
Jenny George, 'Mnemonic'

About the nature of her throat
    could it be a white bird
holding back her name?

About the nature of her chin
    a triangle demands to be alone
aligns to form a question.

About the nature of her sex
    it jives the isle, turns about
snibs on myth of orchard light.

About the nature of her heart
    it truly believes it needs a shape
for such warm and eelish things.

About the nature of her ears
    too featherless to elevate—
cups of dark to travel in.

About the nature of her toes
    they prod against the wall
raise starlight in their caves.

About the nature of her hair
    it tangles in the wind
will not   portrait   her face.

The Bead

Amethyst fell
from my mother's throat–
her birthstone, scattered
in the garden. She'd never
counted her mauve worlds,
couldn't tell if she'd restrung
the frail balance around her neck.
One bead hides in her garden–
observes how the iris
resembles sculpted hair.
Alone and unthreaded,
it calibrates those soft explosions–
jacaranda
jacaranda
jacaranda
Each naked blossom
like a girl snug in her doona–
before she doubted
the properties of mauve.

from **The Guide to Urban Living**

i. *How to hug a tree*

Find the widest patch of parkland,
the longest line of trees.

Walk the path between them,
like a sergeant major—
walk until your rhythm
dissolves
all notions of hierarchy.

Notice how the trunks are spangled
pale green
as if the heartwood
is imagining
how to live at its rim.

Sprawl yourself under a canopy.
Look up, let its green wind
rinse clean through you.

Travel your eyes along each speckled limb,
each tracery of tiny branches,
the internet of green.

Observe how its leaves sift sunlight,
how it sounds like water
running upwards.

Yet, when the sun slips,
a tree empties itself
of light and air, unhitches from the sky.

And binds, densely, to the earth.

Lay your spine down
among its roots, and stay
for as long as you can forget

how to stand up and walk away.

ii. *How to photograph stars*

Yes, light is your enemy.
But it's predictable.

Cities will always
be cluttered with skyglow.

Study NASA's guide
to light pollution:

seek out the darkest places.
You'll find that deserts are reliable.

You must avoid the moon.
Avoid the full moon at all costs.

Get to know your equipment
as if you're a fugitive
and your life depends on it.

Some people will tell you
every star is a word.
Ignore them.

Clarify your intention:
drift of stars or still points?

Set to *Infinity*
then calibrate to a smidgeon before.

Expect the sky to roar with white noise.

Now press the trigger.
Only some will disappear.

iii. *How to draw an iceberg*

Don't be put off by the white
page. Its purity. Icebergs are
not in fact white. Prepare your
full range of blue and green
pencils. And you'll need black:
every iceberg has a shadow
that will help to build shape.
Yes, do your research, but
don't worry. You won't need
to go to Antarctica or Iceland.
Just google. Thousands will
swarm onto your screen. Some
will look like cathedrals; others
like teeth, sharded as a dentist's
nightmare. It's hard to get
the scale right on the page.
I advise that you sketch
in a seal or a dolphin.
Perhaps a rocky ledge.

A Crossing in Iceland

Ísafjörður

There are no zebras in Iceland.
But this one has kick.
White lances
charge the bumper,
pierce my reptilian brain.
Such is the art of the painter.

Perhaps contradiction
pressed my foot to the brake?
Ice melting
cleanly,
casting shadows
so precise, they're robust.

As if darkness can be packaged.
And we are safe as zebras in Iceland.

Deer Child

after *Baby Chair*

by Catherine Woo

The deer child lives aloft
on his own prospective antlers.
I feed him from spoons
carved from maple, birch and apple.

On windless days he's almost flying—
his antlers bud and spiral
down delicate as pencil.

I can't fix a house in the sky
but inside this room
he swings, bucks and teeters—
his antlers barely hold him to the ground.

I want to fill the house
with clouds and mountains.
Ignore the brazen jaws of sunlight.

Glass Lift

(Museum of Contemporary Art, Sydney)

Consider the potential
of passivity. Waiting.

I rely on you
to lead the small things:

when your back touches
mine; when your ear-

shell presses then winces
away—I won't speak.

Some days it's a burden
to only apprehend from inside.

I feel so large to myself.

No one stays
long enough to know

I am blind
to my own window.

I need someone to realise
the view. Please stay.

Outside,
some stars must arrive

in our slice of the sky.
You can translate.

I will protect you from weather.
We can decide.

Are we Jonah and the whale?
Are we of sky, rising like birds?

Are we primate and tree?

Bath

I am like your morning mirror
but won't steal your face—
I am not your self-improvement.

I have no interest in the red
of your skin, how your hairline
limps towards straggle and silver.

In certain lights you'll glimpse
your features slipping
my surface; in my milky depths

your webbed hands, tapered
feet, your pubic hair floating
unguarded as an anemone.

I am amniotic: your heart slows.
Softly, I enter each pore of your skin—
I'm your own warmth distilled.

Sometimes your foot rises above,
as if you want to walk on air—
test the boundary between us.

Then you slide back to me,
breasts, belly and buttocks
at one again with your limbs.

When you break my meniscus—
I reassemble.
My fluidity takes all your space.

Nude

after a photograph of Charis Wilson
by Edward Weston

She is seated like a Degas dancer
but he doesn't care for dance.

Her limbs fold and unfold;
each part more than the whole.

He could not cut off her ear;
it's listening to her knee.

The part-line in her bound hair
hints at an opening.

Is her kneecap the apex
of a secret letter?

Self-Portrait as a Door

a special expression must develop.

Face coated with clay.

Tomas Tranströmer, 'Alone'

You are a fortress, suffering hinges
Aggrieved, again, by your handle.

No tree martyred your making: no
Heartwood nor warps were planed back.

Molten was just a step towards cooling,
Settling to a corpus of ridges & edges.

Your foundations are slipping: gaps
Covet moonlight & dust.

Can you remember when coming
Meant something different to going?

An Argument for the Bee

It's true that variety is manifest
in hummingbirds
but who's to tell how flowers
experience the bee?

And who decreed that joy must be
particular?

Besides, that bird steals
design from flowers.

Must a buzz cancel joy?
A galaxy of migrating butterflies
is said to sound like rain,
yet, when a peacock butterfly
flaps its wings,
you could mistake it for a sneeze.

Hummingbirds breathe
two hundred and fifty
times a minute:
their call, a high-pitched staccato:
surely it's too morse for joy?

They say joy is fleeting,
and I admit,
bees are stalwart,
they rev in second gear,
they make a beeline,
and who feels sparky
as the crow flies?

Joy *scrimaunders,*
and *flinks*: it tumbles butterflies
into contenders.

Yet, consider their biography:
wily as foxes,
they outwitted birds,
reptiles and kittens,
defied the wind and the sun
and the rain.
They climbed mountains,
escaped impalation,
they even spun
their own cocoons.

Yes, joy is floating, buoyant,
but is it self-reliant?

Only the bee
swims inside the flower.

The fox's call is red
and ribboned
in the snow's white shadow.

Robin Robertson, 'What the Horses See at Night'

Six Definitions of Love You Can't Explain

i.
desert wells

ii.
fieldwork with spiritual intent

iii.
music composed on the eyes

iv.
the canvas is larger

v.
a small plane flying
into desert rain

vi.
a pact between red,
blue, and almost white

The Pipe

A great part of every day is not lived consciously. One walks, eats, sees things, deals with what has to be done…
Virginia Woolf, 'Sketch of the Past'

You can never catch the light in your refrigerator when its door is shut. Nor can you catch the man who lives inside it. But somehow, on New Year's Eve, I did. He was wearing white. His hard hat was white. So were his van and the long pipe floating above it in the dusk. His face was soft as if some other version of masculinity had been packed up and sent elsewhere.

'Is this planned work or an emergency?'
'Oh, it's an emergency,' he said.
'What bad timing.'
'Tell me about it,' he said quietly.

We watched the tiny earthmover chew great lumps onto the pavement, each clod collapsing on another. It was somehow monstrous. The man and his white van remained immaculate. Today, the pipe is buried—neat soil packed down on top.

Two Doors Down

If not for the setting
my heart might have
stopped, believing
it was a tiger.
But geranium held sway—
it was a very butch,
very orange,
very battle-
scarred cat.
His back had corrugations
like wet
sand tinted
with volcano,
a thick chocolate
scar
ran the length of his
cheek. His head
brushed planets
and airy lily pads
two feet
above the ground. Still,
he was in proportion—only
imagination sees
a mile wide.

The Super-Salad Emerges from Cellophane

Kale

A studious form of spinach.

Coral growing under water that isn't there:
the more it grows, the more it curls
like well-read books, the more it resembles
a little museum of green.

Purple Cabbage

It has something of William Morris
but is hard as Brighton Rock.

Unsettling as stripey flowers
and paperchains that border classrooms:
something is wrong
when festive combines with neat.

Beetroot

A creature drawn from a small black lake.

A vegetarian dreams her version of black pudding.

Breasts under wine-dark lycra, or speaking
from the table I've-left-your-body womb.
Yes, beetroot is the new black.

Profile

We joke about relationship
as commodity,
hide our ragged hearts,
but where's the guide to choose
the one you'd want to save before your cat?
Discard those who erase themselves
with landscape, shades, a hat.
Wonder about portraits cropped
from curves of a lover,
those in locked embrace
with their mother.
Try not to imagine yourself there,
up to your elbows, kneeling, in your underwear.
Forget the ones who seek style,
a sense of humour, must be tactile, intelligent
and never lose her temper.
What's to love about staying calm,
fixing things around the house?
And if you were sent to me, my love,
would I find that hat a trifle ostentatious,
those stripes too particular, your gaze far
too penetrating.

Conversation with an Optometrist

Chin up. Chin up.
That's it. Now, look right between my eyes.

If you ever get sick of this job, you would be a good carpenter.

Or an engineer. Engineers are always our fussiest customers.
With engineers it is always about...

Precision?

Yes, and the way things work.
They look good.
They have a nice, refined line.
How do they feel?

They hurt.

I guess it comes down to fashion versus comfort.

Oh, my vanity evaporated long ago.

Chin up. Chin up.

A memory of blue eyes.

Things Your Mother Never Tells You

My son, my son, I love the careless
    grace of you. Your milky skin,
your midnight hair, the sweep
    as it falls on my arm as you sleep.
That soft blood, your mouth,
    it blossoms on your face,
too wide and bold to be a rose.
    Your eyes are strokes in the art of you,
calligraphy as ancient as sleep.
    I love your long toes like piano keys,
straight as your teeth, a tuned
    kind of symmetry of feet. My son,
you have harp toes, lute toes, they strum
    on air—
            igniting songs for your leap.

The Night Before the Truck

A medley of cutlery and utensils crowd the table;
a stockpot's orange lid cosies in; they're hoboes in limbo—
this week, a kind of wake for all the food and drink
that's passed over; all the times you kicked
your foot against my leg—
Now, a mop, a bucket, an army of boxes
assemble near the entrance. Army's incorrect;
they're far from organised, more like hippies
gathered for folksong at the door.
O the comfort of constructing lists, yet in you flop
upon my bed, wondering if all you need
is the black box that connects
you to everything, and the archive of your sketchbooks.
I could live inside that colander: it's dark and round
and sturdy, more than half a world,
flecked with tiny holes, so many rooms—
full of air and vagrancy.

Dodge, 1960

The name skips with mischief,
but its pink's entirely
still. Droplets cling to long machismo,
reinvent the rain,
a case for girlish innocence,
and cherry blossom, breaking through—
snarling down the highway.
Could engine turn to timpani,
then a self-effacing hum?
Better not underestimate
the possibilities for pink.
Triumphant, gleaming,
somehow powdery,
even in the rain. No one
could mistake that paint
for undercoat—
unless one believes
rose lingerie undressed.

His Grey Suit

In the warehouse it began to get cool when dusk set in. He offered me his suit coat to wear over my white lace dress. And so I slipped it on. It was like wearing a grey silk kimono, only warmer. He told me it is his first ever suit. He wears it often now. 'I love wearing it, I don't know why I haven't worn one for years, I can feel it shift like silk against my legs. The man fixed the length of the trousers with barely two hours to spare before the funeral. He took such care. Have you lost your mother? You will really feel it. I knew when she had gone. I felt her leave my body. I was in the kitchen cutting onions and I felt this haiku arrive: *stirring the onions/ my mother is dead*. And I felt her leave. Ten minutes later I got the call to tell me she was dead.'

Anaphora

Grief is like a pair of socks,
enveloping
as a second skin.
Your feet can keep
the socks together.
Step, step, step.
Dress them in hard leather.

Grief is like a pair of socks.
Come day's end,
wear marks
fragile in the weft.
Reveal one pair
to be the same
as all the others.

Grief is like a pair of socks,
very often black.
Sometimes dove-grey
can tip the toes as if
pointing somewhere
beyond
another yawning night.

Grief is like a pair of socks.
Take them off.
Place one inside
the other. Hold them
between your palms—
confront your orphaned feet.

How similar fingers are to toes.
How similar hands to feet.
How similar love to grief.

Ricochet

four foxes chase a calf
until its legs tip over   foxes—
they chew cow ears don't they?
he found a clutch of tags behind his shed
he said *the foxes*   cried when a deer released her fawn
behind his shed   four foxes   red fire engines.
merry christmas to you and you
let children ride high through rural streets—who calls
emergency and why?   90% of infected rabbits
die   four foxes   red fire engines   a howl
of sirens somewhere   he held a mouse with shattered wings—
sheltered it   inside his hand   they catch
in ceiling fans   only kindness   left to do   four foxes   red
fire engines   a howl of sirens   they called her
a fucking moll   four foxes   blue tags—
red   a howl

Forgetfulness

I taste it because I resist winter bees. I taste it because I really love snow. I taste it because fresh water consoles more than salt. I taste it because no one unpacks every ant, every sting. I taste it because it makes words breed silk on my tongue. I taste it because secrets buzz loud as a hive.

I taste it because memory infects every sentence. I taste it because islands are underrated. I taste it because replay blisters like experience. I taste it because a mantis stuck to the glass—stepped her mint-green into the clutch of a dust-weary web. I taste it because I slither and left cells of my skin. I taste it because waking prepares for more dreaming. I taste it to snap off my shadow.

Fire is a Strange Craftsman

after *The Arsonist*
by Chloe Hooper

He likes the burning patterns.
And flames have infinite shapes. His heart
seems to drown in them.

It was almost like a sunrise.
Like someone waving an orange blanket above my head.
There were embers the size of dinner plates.
Embers the size of pillows.
I was pelted by burning gumnuts.

It was like the air *was* red.
There was no air in the air.
It was like sucking on a hairdryer.
Like seven jumbos landing on the roof.

Burning birds fell from the trees,
igniting the ground where they landed.
Everything started to shake. I was picked up off my feet.
Like seven jumbos landing on the roof.

Everything went blood red. You could not get the depth
of how far this red fell.

As if the house was picked up and thrown
into a sea of fire.
Windows started to crack. Skylights melted.
He went out into the inferno with a gun and shot his horses.

It got dark so fucking quickly.
Darker than night.
I could not see where the house was.
The breathing tube in my facemask melted
and liquid plastic burnt my lips.

He likes the burning patterns.
And flames have intimate shapes. His heart
kind of drowns there.

when does a flower begin forging its weapon
Yi Lu, 'Carnation'

To the Goth Girl Sketching Lotus

Royal Botanic Gardens, Melbourne 30.12.2022

May your black boots skim
   the lake's ballet,
   your fingers channel
   phantoms of pink
   and elfin green.

May you sonar
   fields of failing parachutes—
   dive the darkness,
   travel the sway
   of drowned roots.

May you grasp
   the toxic tarantella,
   gasp, vector your night-
   vison. Be deft, be agile.
   Return torn lotus to the lake.

A Wake of Marigolds

i.m. Retta Hemensley

If a riot could knit, it might
assemble blooms that look like this:

raucous yellows, livid golds,
burnt or burning orange.

Did you know they're edible?
So full of sun, a midnight snack

would have to taste upside down.
I'd been expecting detonations:

saffron, chilli and paprika,
not this muffled honey.

Yesterday, I found them breaking
through my neighbour's fence.

Now, they constellate
in wooden boxes outside the Bot Café—

treasure boxes, their lids flung open—
caffeine for the eyes.

Impossible as your dying.

Carnations

She wanted poppies.
Wanted their every which way.
But at her bedside, the vase
brandishes carnations: their thicket
of ball-and-socket stems
remind of prosthetic limbs.

Strange that carnations
escaped the fate of roses.
No one says your lips
are luscious as carnations.

Pinks, her grandma called them:
to pierce, puncture, stab.

Each petal scratches its toothy edges,
recalling all things carnation—
from the Latin *caro:*
flesh, the colour of the flower.

Perhaps resistance is bred
into this flower—soft serrations
don't invite embrace—a legacy
from that shepherd boy
who dared to turn Diana down.

She tore out his eyes, flung
them to the ground.
Now they're warriors
marshalling in hospitals.
Some could survive the patients.

She imagines wild carnations
in sunlight,
their velvet rising—
dark burgundy
over lines and lines of foliage.

Blue Reports from the Field

I'm content in delphiniums, the knitted-eyes of cornflowers.
So why must I inject into the depths of *every* flower?

I'm already the underlay of heather on late afternoons.
At certain times of day, I coexist with stars.

Don't complain. I always make room for the moon.
I am blue, objecting. Blue Moon is just a song.

So take your jackhammer underground, extract
my lapis lazuli, disrupt my veins of sapphire.

You can pretend I'm distilled in your hand.
I'll sequester your lips then blow every pore blue.

I am Learning Peacefulness

I almost miss her.
Told to look for 'massive tributes',
there are none.

Only a tumble of blue and pink
so voluminous
it covers up her name.

There are no poppies in October.
It's borage and granny's bonnet in June.

Snapdragons, and low-growing lemon
roses enfold her edges.

Bees come and go with a soft burr
that sounds like honey.

A single strand of sedge rides the air—
slow Ariel.

Releasing the Poppies

Despite its vital place in the mythology and visual culture of war, its unpredictable and short lifespan means it has no place in a formal planting system.
Paul Gough,
'Seed, soil, sapling: reflections on the flowers of war and peace'

i. *Uninvited*

Yes, grass is ruthless.
But poppies, unaware,
happen uninvited.
Raising crinkled crimson faces,
those fringed eyes
don't know how to flinch.
Their buds droop
like old men's chins.
Recall the mood of certain gods
and crush them.

ii. *Iceland poppies*

Too soft-boned to hold up their heads,
they're lanky children spilling
over metal buckets.
Their eyes are yellow-green.
Vegetable eyes.
Vegetable hearts.
They speak pear, peach and apricot.
Someone's committing a slow
erasure of red.
In Iceland, no one complains.

iii. *A room of white poppies*

after *War Room*
by Cornelia Parker

The poppies have flown—
sent to new homes: lapels,
wreaths, assorted hats.

Some vitrine in cellophane,
breathless—
uncertain of their destination.

Only their stencils remain,
draping us in tepid red.

So many white poppies,
each the same:
cookie-cutter cannon-fodder.

Our eyes are filled with white
poppies—
demobbed and breaking
us open.

iv. *Opium*

Their relatives are outlaws.
They'll resist
even the mildest edit–
pretend they've never heard
of flowerbeds.

Expect their stems to bristle,
loop and bend
as if itching to invade the sky.

They'll eclipse
your pumpkins: gypsy magentas,
dervish pinks, a glaucous red
shimmering
a catastrophe of silver.

Unlike the Dutch masters,
you don't get to choose.

Light's roulette could toss
out a burgundy
or blotchy mauves.

'Mrs Perry' could errant white–
add bruise to her complexion.

Take your chances.
Fling yourself into their axes.

v. *When poppies close at night*

Stories slip in with them;
they tremble
in scarlet capes as woodsmen drip
the bedroom red;
they begin to swallow oceans,
become the apple
and the mirror;
suddenly double-petalled,
they imagine
what it's like to endure
like a rose: to receive a title
from men compelled to cultivate
a single flower.
Emboldened, they commune
with beasts,
forget their seven brothers.
Clotted with dreams,
they wake
again, to wear time's work.

vi. *Coquelicot*

A shade of red. From a vernacular term
for the wild corn poppy (Fr.)

We do not feed wild birds,
nor depend on wind to propagate,
we are ourselves   slow wind—
ripples—
            the unfolding
                        of a meadow.

And the kangaroo settles down, pronged,
then lifts itself
carefully, like a package passed over with both hands—

Robert Gray, 'The Dusk'

Coral

You are not a metropolis built for hummingbirds,
but you could be jungles blooming from stone.

You don't play solitaire like buttons of anemone,
though you do belong in their archive.

You believe in free love as if born in the 60s,
abandoning yourself to all manner of algae.

Flowerchild, you are growing communities,
bonding, even in death. Your skeletons

spindle upwards and outwards. You'll never
read Darwin nor Dickens, but you could be

Miss Havisham's long bridal bouquet—
waiting for water to cool, algae to enter your flesh.

You'll never fragrance like *agave amica*
nor leap like a lemur—hibiscus splashing your ear.

Unlike the fish, movement (even allowing
for slow time) will never be your forte.

You are not the crowns of volcanoes
but you are their lost shadows.

On windless days you rewrite
the Garden of Eden, fluoresce like auroras.

For coral are flower animals.
And like crows we pick over your bones.

Clocking Stars

Magnolia stellata

Why does it stand
blooming like a supernova,
dropping bright litter in winter
as though it's autumn?

Every star is broken.
Every white, rimmed brown.
Their light congeals,
each petal almost succulent.

Do tethered stars learn early
they must embrace
their falling?

*

The tree is in fast-forward
and the sky is gaslight-blue.
Winter light should stem
the flow—yet doesn't.

Furry buds are pressing
beside each slurred star.
How the bees love
this honey before it's made.

Night bees leave their hives,
descend upon magnolia.
I must go home
and plant my bee box in the ground.

Beyond 87.8° Fahrenheit

If the eggs incubate above 87.8° Fahrenheit

...the hatchlings will be female.

National Ocean Service, US Department of Commerce

She does not remember
the day nor month of her birth.

Yet, from when the world began,
history was written on her back.

Her shell was sought for divination—
constellations troubled her dome.

Viewed from underneath,
a swimming turtle could be flying.

Once, I saw her orbit the moon.

But a tiny hole drilled in her bone
tethers her to misery.

Her shell was a sounding board
for lutes, harps and mandolins.

Miry ointment from her brain
was said to cure squinting.

She adapted human eyes
to see beneath her carapace.

Her gaze insists its slivered stars.
And numbers are writing her back.

The Trespass of Deer

Deer can shatter their reflection, shake the boy immersed in pixels—
send him leaping upstairs to phone his father.

It is easy to be kind to deer when they stand on crags in Scottish paintings.
She's never seen a wild one, but they've always been with her—

silhouettes in forests as she turns each coloured page.
A trick imparting distance.

Her uncle tracks them, scopes them with a gun. He skins and cleaves them;
gifts their haunches raw or roasted with trimmings. They trespass.

The farmers and the Greens stand united: *not in my backyard.*
Bishop, safe inside a bus, grasped the exquisite visitation of a moose.

She never wrestled with a deer. Miles out at sea, three fishermen
lugged up a deer: *his big sad eyes* were shining in the dark.

Lost Oyster Buoys

If you're on the water or around the edge of the bays you may notice some stray oyster buoys. The buoys can break free in rough weather…
The Coastal Column, January 2024

Any boy will wander when given half a chance.
Oyster buoys
are no exception: every tide-tug, every cord-stretch,
a provocation.
Let's leave gender aside. Many young things oppose
the expected.
And what a sorry existence: mapping those creatures
that fatten
inside their casement—lacking even a sketchy concept
of straying.
Oysters. After all their quiet dreaming in emperor dark,
the shock
of what they are. Alive, exposed to air, quivering.
Their home
a frozen wave of white when every fibre knew it black.
The blade
nothing compared with this shucked light.

Theft of Bone

i. *Unspecified bone*

Sudden artefact
the bones are clean
and polished by sun.

Each piece so intact
invites a mapping, knowing,
naming.

Such lack–
how to place it back together–
is it wallaby or rabbit?

Unease palpates–
each bone existing
amid collapse of structure.

ii. *Bird skull*

Years ago, I found a skull
sun-warmed in a pocket of dune.

How easy to take part of a bird.

Up close, its beak venerable
as an ancient's beard.

Bone-husk: I knew it once held
the beads of a perceiving mind.

The delicacy terrified.
Each absence fiercely bird.

iii. *Antlers*

Did you know
antlers are made of bone?

Centuries ago, when burnt to ash
they formed a paint called hartshorn white.

Last night, I dreamt an albino deer
startled from the mirror. I wore her fur,

hung my head in the entrance hall.
I like to wear my antlers most of the time now.

Hydra

after the sculpture
The Ferry Captain, a Rhyll Maritime Story
by Brandon Kroon

Of course, I always knew that life must end.
All those years colliding with salted-wind,
stretching my limbs to their limit, my fronds
somewhere between barnacles and rind—
watching the jetty dissolve to drier grey.
I'd witnessed raw wood hauled in, heard
the sawing and the planing as hulls assembled
like giant seeds. I'd tracked each boat
returning, releasing netted silver—
frantic, then neatly dead. It was the calm
reason after the storm that shook my core.
Council decreed a part of me might break
a human life. Now, I'm that many-headed monster:
captain companioned by those creatures clubbed,
shot or otherwise made still: seal, swan,
pelican and fish. Shorn by chainsaw's blade,
we are kin, rooted to the earth—our glaze
conversing with the weather.

Deconstructing Yes

Posters bloomed yellow, red &
black on picket fences. Jasmine
& geranium crept towards the YES.

Wisteria draped its mauve
cascade along a tall pine fence:
the lilac YES almost blended in.

She spied YES masquerading
as the painting of a sunrise,
curated on a builder's cyclone fence.

Some neighbours flared two posters
on their borders (often a double block).
Would they WRITE YES twice?

It was rare for apartments
to sport a YES.
Did tenants have to seek permission?

Every morning, she debated:
which YES was most convincing?

VOTE YES was bossy.
WRITE YES was less bossy
& she always liked a homophone.

Then, YES YES appeared
on the window of a local shop
(one bright gold, the other red).

They'd left their tools of trade
on the table: measure-tape,
needles & spools of thread.

Now, YES is upside down,
propped beside a flyscreen door.

The Border

after the Bieszczady Mountains

The truck, all blue melting into rust—mutters down the narrow track through fields so wide they seem to float, slows over unbridged streams, and there is time to be undone by grass and trees stubborn as history. The truck conjoins a daisied fence, men commune along a bench, slosh vodka into jars break the hunt with cleavers. The mountain seethes in red and brown: its eye so fierce even sheep fear to graze here—forest slips beneath feet, children cluster behind stones. Once, I saw a horse and dray, heading east through afternoon, as if *after* was still unresolved.

The Justice of Grass

Morning breaks
its green chandelier
and I am walking
through grass,

in what I thought
was a buffer zone.

Yet, under my feet,
a runway
disappears
in different directions.

One crow
and two silver gulls
herald
with form and call—

scoping, yes,
but I am not their prey,
nor collateral
from any specious drone.

Security here is worse
than on any golf course
in Florida.

Did someone build
this airfield
entirely for birds?

It's so vast.
So uninterrupted.

One horizon reaches
towards sounding ocean,
the other towards
a road cutting inland.

Is there a field small enough
for a human to bear it?

Dusk at Cape Woolamai

you enter through shoulders of sand
    riffles of sprawling grasses
            shadows lean into vans
    surfboards stowed
or removed   the rhythm so relaxed
    so loose at its edges
            you can't tell who is coming or leaving

some evenings your blood
    is calm as the weather   walking aligns
            with gazing and breathing
    your lungs hold horizons and clifftops
and waves bring stones to your feet
    thin and concentric
            as if they have nothing to defend

foam is sliding your feet
    you could walk the tideline
            forever   be nothing
    but sky   milky sea   spill of sunset
mirrored on sand   last surfers
    are skimming the waves
            you rinse and rinse in mauve-red

until plovers skitter forward
    dwarfing water and sand
            you slowly ascend
    sinking ankle-deep   retracing to where
silhouettes slip into men
    others keel into boys   skid their wheels
            as if the road is a vagrant wave

A Bowerbird, Forgetting Blue

is outrageous. Unthinkable. Yet the idea caught in my mind a few weeks after you left this world. It returned when I walked the shore of Cape Woolamai, recalling the fluther of *Velella velella*, its washup at the tideline in early December: its glitter, its blue phosphorescence. As if a bowerbird had been set loose by the sea.

It's tempting to open the cage of a bird when you are gazing out at the sea. Every atom feels porous, already blown through. Down here, I've always suspected that we are made up of almost nothing. The physicist on Radio National merely confirmed it, explaining how the gap between each atom's core and its electron wave is akin to a sparrow flying the Sistine Chapel. Would a bowerbird set loose by the sea survive? Could it learn from the sea: how to disperse, how to let go, how to give over the bower?

It was colder in April. I took shelter by the cliff face that falls down to the sea. The volcanic rock is sculpted—blue-grey washed in copper, pitted and patterned—loops that join up with each other. How to read the slow stories of stones? I got tired of trying to decide if it was a kind of frozen-emergence, a kind of pre-meaning

And then I saw it. A lone by-the-wind sailor caught on the shelf of rock. A feather had landed in the same hollow, its quill lugged in a pool of sand. This *Velella velella* had no hint of blue, not even at its rim. It was no longer moist. It was an oval mandala, traced precisely, resisting the nothing. It was milky, slightly sticky, resistant to pressure from my finger. It dilated O so slightly. It almost took a breath. It was pinned by its sail, fluttering.

Notes

The epigraphs to Part I and 'She' are by Jenny George.
Jenny George, excerpts from 'Intelligence' and 'Mnemonic' from *The Dream of Reason*. Copyright © 2018 by Jenny George. Reprinted with the permission of The Permissions Company, LLC on behalf of Copper Canyon Press, coppercanyonpress.org.

'The Deer Woman' is after the bronze sculpture *Born* (2002) by Kiki Smith Buffalo AKG Art Museum, New York.

'ii. *How to photograph stars*' in '*from* The Guide to Urban Living' is adapted from fragments of text found in 'Tutorial: How to take photos of the stars – part 1' by the Polish photographer Wojciech Toman: http://hdrphotographer.blogspot.com.au and is used with permission.
'*every star is a word*' is a minor adaptation of 'each star is a word' from 'The Path of Least Resistance' by Mary Ruefle (*The Adamant*, University of Iowa Press, Iowa City, 1989).

'A Crossing in Iceland': the pedestrian crossing in Ísafjörður is designed to slow traffic by creating an optical illusion of floating above the road.

'Deer Child' is after the sculpture *Baby Chair* by Tasmanian-based artist Catherine Woo. Signs of Progress (solo exhibition), Arc One Gallery, Melbourne, 2024.

'Nude' is after the photograph of Charis Wilson by Edward Weston titled *Nude* (1936). Prints are owned by a number of public institutions including The Museum of Modern Art, New York.

'Self-Portrait as a Door' borrows its title from a poem in *Bestiary*, Donika Kelly (Graywolf Press, 2016).

'Self-Portrait as a Door': the epigraph is from 'Alone' by Tomas Tranströmer. Tranströmer, Tomas. *New Collected Poems*, trans. Robin Fulton (Bloodaxe Books, 2011) www.bloodaxebooks.com. Reprinted with permission.

'An Argument for the Bee': *Scrimaunder*: to wander about, take a devious or winding course (Yorkshire dialect). *Flinks*: to ramble in a rompish manner (Shetland dialect). These words, along with their definition and origin, are from 'Glossary V: Underlands', in Robert MacFarlane's, *Landmarks* (Hamish Hamilton, 2015).

Part II: the epigraph is from 'What the Horses See at Night' by Robin Robertson. Robertson, Robin. *Sailing the Forest: Selected Poems* (Picador, 2014).

'Six Definitions of Love You Can't Explain' is adapted from 'Colouring the Desert' by Nicholas Rothwell, *The Weekend Australian*. July 20, 2013.

'The Pipe': the epigraph is from 'Sketch of the Past' by Virginia Woolf (manuscript 1939–1940). Woolf, Virginia. *Moments of Being: Autobiographic Writings*, ed. Jeanne Schulkind (Pimlico, 2002).

'His Grey Suit': the haiku 'stirring the onions/ my mother is dead' is by Matt Hetherington. The poem was inspired by a conversation with him on December 11, 2012 and is published with permission.

'Forgetfulness': 'I taste it because' is from Mona Arshi's 'Taster', *Small Hands* (Liverpool University Press, 2015), 'to snap off my shadow' is adapted from 'my shadow is snapped off' in 'Crabs' by Sam Meekings, *The Bestiary* (Polygon, 2008).

'Fire is a Strange Craftsman' draws from *The Arsonist,* Chloe Hooper, (Penguin, 2008). Stanzas 1 and 8 comprise adapted fragments from 'Part 3: The Courtroom'. The title and stanzas 2–7 are constructed from text (found, some with minor adaptations) in 'Part 1: The Detectives'; includes some of the many anonymous witness statements.

Part III: the epigraph is from 'Carnation' by Yi Lu.
Yi Lu, excerpt from 'Carnation', translated by Fiona Sze-Lorrain, from *Sea Summit: Poems*. Translation copyright © 2015 by Fiona Sze-Lorrain. Reprinted with the permission of The Permissions Company LLC on behalf of Milkweed Editions, Milkweed.org.

'To the Goth Girl Sketching Lotus': the title was influenced by those in Anna Jacobson's *The Last Postman* (Vagabond Press, 2018).

'I am Learning Peacefulness': the title is from 'Tulips' by Sylvia Plath (*Ariel*, Faber and Faber, 1965).

'Releasing the Poppies': epigraph by Paul Gough is from Seed, soil, sapling: reflections on flowers of war and peace. July 2019 *Critical Military Studies* 6 (1) 1–4.

'iii. *A room of white poppies*' in 'Releasing the Poppies' is after *War Room* (2015) by the British artist Cornelia Parker. This installation was exhibited in 2019 at the Museum of Contemporary Art Australia, Sydney.

'iv. *Opium*' in 'Releasing the Poppies': 'Mrs Perry' is a pink variety of the oriental poppy (*Papaver oriental*) from which a white arrived. It was cultivated and named 'Perry's White'. It has striking dark-purple central blotches.

Part IV: the epigraph is from 'The Dusk' by Robert Gray.
Gray, Robert. *Grass Script* (Angus & Robertson, 1979). Reprinted with permission.

'The Trespass of Deer': the line 'Bishop, safe inside a bus, grasped the exquisite visitation of a moose' is a reference to 'The Moose' by Elizabeth Bishop, *The Complete Poems, 1927–1979*. (Farrax, Strauss and Giroux, New York, 1980). A decade or more ago, Oddspot in *The Age* reported that three ocean fishermen drew up an adult deer in their net. The outcome was not reported.

'Lost Oyster Buoys': the epigraph is from an advertisement published in the January 2024 edition of *The Coastal Column*, Scamander, Tasmania.

'Hydra' is after the chainsaw sculpture *The Ferry Captain, a Rhyll Maritime Story* by Brandon Kroon (2019). It was carved from a cypress pine on the Rhyll foreshore after it was damaged by a storm in 2016. Historic details of Phillip Island were found from a variety of sources including: 'From Silver to Sponges, the Industries that Built the Island', *Phillip Island & San Remo Advertiser*, 15 February 2022.

'The Border' was inspired by the Polish crime drama *The Border*. Filmed in the Bieszczady Mountains, it is set near the border with Ukraine. Parts of this mountain range also fall within the borders of Ukraine and Slovenia. The mountains have witnessed many battles including many along the Eastern Front of World War I.

'The Justice of Grass': title is adapted from 'the thin justice of grass' in 'Resistance' by Traci Brimhall (*Poetry*, February 2019).

'iii. *Antlers*' in 'Theft of Bone': 'hung my head in the entrance hall' is adapted from 'hung my head on the kitchen wall' in 'Portrait of My Whiteness as a Deer' by Katie Hale (*White Ghosts*, Nine Arches Press, 2023). The last line is a minor adaptation of 'I too wear my antlers most of the time/now', 'Chimeras' by Brian Sneeden (*Poetry*, July/August 2024).

Acknowledgements

A number of these poems, some in earlier versions, have appeared in the following journals and newspapers: *Antipodes: A Global Journal of Australian/New Zealand Literature* (USA), *Axon, Cordite, Hecate, Meanjin, Meniscus, Not Very Quiet, The Canberra Times, The Weekend Australian.*

Some poems appear or are forthcoming in these anthologies: *100 Poets* (Flying Island Books, 2025), *Best of Australian Poems* (Australian Poetry, 2025), *Brushstrokes* (WA Poets Inc., 2025), *Equinox and Sky Gazing* (Poets Choice, USA, 2024), *Family Matters: An International Anthology* (Nivasini Publishers, India, 2014), *Wingspan* (Puncher & Wattmann, 2026), *Grieve Volume 11* (Hunters Writer Centre, 2024), *In Your Hands* (Red Room Company, 2020), *Joy: poems from the 2017 ACU prize for poetry* (Australian Catholic University Press, 2017), *Oystercatcher Two: 101 Poems* (Five Islands Press, 2025), *Remnants: an anthology of microlit* (Spineless Wonders, 2024), *Resilience: a celebration of poetry, fiction and essays from Mascara Literary Review* (Ultimo Press, 2022), *Ricochet: an anthology of microlit* (Spineless Wonders, 2025).

'The Night Before the Truck' and 'His Grey Suit' (the latter under a different title) were first published in *The Earthing of Rain* (bilingual) translated by Iris Fan Xing (Flying Island Books, 2019).

'His Grey Suit' is part of the prose-poem sequence 'On the Other Side of Love', Commended in the 2013 FAW John Shaw Neilson Poetry Award.

'An Argument for the Bee' was Highly Commended in the 2017 Australian Catholic University Poetry Prize.

'The Night Before the Truck' was equal runner-up in the 2017 NSW Society of Women Writers National Poetry Prize.

'The Border' was a finalist in the 2024 Joanna Burns Microlit Award.

'Anaphora' was longlisted in the 2024 Grieve Project.

'Forgetfulness' was a finalist in the 2025 Joanna Burns Microlit Award.

'Coral' was shortlisted in the 2025 Inaugural Robert Gray Poetry Prize.

'Carnations' was longlisted in the 2025 Ros Spencer Poetry Prize.

Grateful acknowledgement is made to the publishers, editors and judges.

My loving gratitude to Debbie Lim who critiqued many individual poems and offered valuable suggestions for the manuscript. Warmest thanks to Bonny Cassidy for her incisive critique of the manuscript. Warmest thanks to Charles D'Anastasi, Alex Skovron and the late Ron Pretty for their critique of particular poems. Many thanks to Matt Hetherington who instantly gave permission to include his haiku in 'His Grey Suit'. I am grateful to Dapeng Liu for his collaboration and kind permission to use his artwork. I feel blessed by the warm and expert support from my editor and publisher Terri-ann White.

About Upswell

Upswell Publishing was established in 2021 by Terri-ann White as a not-for-profit press. A perceived gap in the market for distinctive literary works in fiction, poetry and narrative non-fiction was the motivation. In her years as a bookseller, writer and then publisher, Terri-ann has maintained a watch on literary books and the way they insinuate themselves into a cultural space and are then located within our literary and cultural inheritance. She is interested in making books to last: books with the potential to still be noticed, and noted, after decades and thus be ripe to influence new literary histories.

About this typeface

Book designer Becky Chilcott chose Foundry Origin not only as a strong, carefully considered, and dependable typeface, but also to honour her late friend and mentor, type designer Freda Sack, who oversaw the project. Designed by Freda's long-standing colleague, Stuart de Rozario, much like Upswell Publishing, Foundry Origin was created out of the desire to say something new.

www.ingramcontent.com/pod-product-compliance
Ingram Content Group Australia Pty Ltd
76 Discovery Rd, Dandenong South VIC 3175, AU
AUHW021412150426
425928AU00002B/3